THE LAMB AND THE FÜHRER

JESUS TALKS WITH HITLER

RAVI ZACHARIAS

MULTNOMAH
BOOKS

THE LAMB AND THE FÜHRER

Published in association with the literary agency of Wolgemuth & Associates, Inc.,
8600 Crestgate Circle, Orlando, FL 32819
© 2005 by Ravi Zacharias
International Standard Book Number: 978-1-60142-320-7

Published in the United States by Multnomah, an imprint of the Crown Publishing
Group, a division of Penguin Random House LLC, New York.

MULTNOMAH® and its mountain colophon are registered trademarks of
Penguin Random House LLC.

Printed in the United States of America

Library of Congress Cataloging-in-Publication Data
Zacharias, Ravi K.
   The lamb and the Führer : Jesus talks with Hitler / Ravi Zacharias.
     p. cm. — (Great conversations)
   ISBN 1-59052-394-6
   1. Jesus Christ—Fiction. 2. Hitler, Adolf, 1889-1945—Fiction. 3. Imaginary
conversations. I. Title. II. Series.
   PS3576.A19L36 2005
   813'.54—dc22

                              2005017525

To
Stuart McAllister
Friend and colleague to help make
this world a better place

ACKNOWLEDGMENTS

I would like to thank my colleague Stuart McAllister, who was my guide and resource in research as I studied the man who ushered in the Third Reich and irremediably changed the history of the world. Stuart was patient and an invaluable source of information. I am deeply grateful to him. Without him I could not have attempted this project.

Then there is my son, Nathan, who encouraged me and traveled with me to touch my heart with the reality that this subject has a deep impact even for his generation. For them I sought some answers. Thanks as always to my wife, Margie, for doing the edits and helping with ideas from her own reading, because she is far more knowledgeable in the history of this period than I am.

My heartfelt thanks also goes to Rod Morris for the advice and the finishing touch in his edits.

Introduction

"I want to raise a generation of young people, imperious, relentless, and cruel." With these words, Adolf Hitler spilled the blood of millions of people, his own as well as others, when he set himself as a god in the minds of his people. He pursued his dream and unleashed a hell upon the earth. As I traveled through the sites of the carnage of the Second World War, I was reminded afresh of the horror and the extent of human pain and suffering inflicted on so many by one man and those willing to follow him. The concentration camps, the Gestapo offices, and the gas ovens still speak today of the incalculable price that was paid. Any words that try to describe it become dwarfed because the story is monstrous.

There is no name today more synonymous with power, wickedness, and unprecedented violence than his. But nearly two thousand years before him, another walked this earth whose name is symbolic of love, peace, and life. His was a name also associated with the spilling of blood—His own, shed for the sake of the world. He endured hell to open the way to heaven. What would a conversation between these two be like? There were voices in Hitler's day that tried to stop him. One was Dietrich Bonhoeffer, a

German pastor, who went so far as to be part of a plot to assassinate Hitler. Bonhoeffer believed that for the sake of the world, Hitler had to be removed, and he paid for that conviction with his life.

In this conversation that we imagine between Jesus and Hitler, Bonhoeffer joins in because he brings into focus the reality of the struggle that good men and women faced under national socialism. Violence, racism, power, lies, death, philosophy, evil are all given a face here. But then there is the face of love, individual worth, supreme goodness, power, truth, peace, and life in Jesus Christ. In the face of Bonhoeffer we see anguish, helplessness, and a will to change evil for good.

It was not difficult to find Hitler's own words of self-justification for his actions. It was not that difficult either to find Bonhoeffer's words that described the soul struggle he faced. But what would Jesus have said when ethics comes into conflict with an ethic that chose to kill to stop the killing? That part was harder, and it is in those words alone that the huge reality of these issues can be grasped.

So enter with me into Hitler's bunker and listen in as the Führer, gun in hand, is about to end his life (synonymous in his mind with Germany itself), knowing that his Third Reich did not last a thousand years or bring a Final Solution, but in fact resulted in the destruction of his own country and much of Europe. How could good people have followed such an evil man? What is the origin of such violence? How does blood recompense for blood? Listen as Jesus, Hitler, and Bonhoeffer engage in a life-and-death discussion.

It is my earnest hope that, in a world now full of violence, the voice of Jesus will be heard again calling men and women to submit to His sacrifice so that we will not continue to sacrifice our own sons and daughters on the battlefields of human ego and ideological conflict.

THE LAMB AND THE FÜHRER

JESUS TALKS WITH HITLER

Daniel: It's hard to imagine now, isn't it? Just debris. But underneath here was his actual bunker?

Erik: Yes. Until one comes here and sees that nothing remains, you don't realize that the destruction was so thorough. Everything was razed. I mean, the Russians were within half a mile when he decided to end it all. Bombs, shelling, shooting, memos…"the end is coming"…"they are here." In one sense it's too bad, really. When you go to England, you can see Churchill's cabinet war rooms left almost exactly the way they were when the war ended.

Daniel: But here in Berlin, all is stones and dirt.

Erik: Even though it was his last stand, I'm afraid there is very little of the Reich's physical presence that remains. But there is something that somehow was spared. When we're finished here, let's drive to that most cultured of all German cities, Nuremberg. It's a little over two hundred miles from here, which won't take long on the autobahn. The Hall of Justice still stands intact and functions as a courthouse. But here in Berlin, you just have to step back for a moment and try to picture it as it was. See this "hall of shame" we're walking past? This is where the Gestapo headquarters was. Can you imagine the fear and terror that haunted these halls? And the so-called "People's Court" that was neither for the people nor really a court. It was a gathering of robed and uniformed people with the power to kill without feeling. It is rightly called the "Topography of Terror." A memorial site is planned here in the future. But let's move on to Nuremberg.

Daniel: Boy! You guys don't have any speed limits here, do you? That fellow who just streaked past was a blur!

Erik: Ja! We don't like driving in America. It's like putting your car in reverse. I mean, why do you design a car to do such speeds and then just crawl along at fifty-five or sixty miles an hour? It's like going backwards in time.

Daniel: I know, Erik, but as my dad used to say—the faster you move, the farther ahead you should be able to see.

Erik: I've driven with your dad. He didn't have to see very far, did he?

Daniel: No, but I don't think he expects to see the Autobahns in heaven, either. And while you're in the mood to hit us Americans, can we stop for lunch, please? And not another Wiener schnitzel! A good old MacDonald's would be very welcome.

Erik: You can take the boy out of—

Daniel: Okay, okay. Some more breaded veal down the hatch. I guess when the Russians arrived, there wasn't much choice between the cuisines, was there?

Erik: Enough out of you. Here we are. This is Nuremberg. Did you see the movies about the trial?

Daniel: I saw *Judgment at Nuremberg*, which was about the judges who supported the Nazi regime being placed on trial. The closing statement of the chief justice is worth sitting through every minute of that three-hour movie for.

Erik: Yes, and *Nuremberg*, which is powerful and quite accurate, was about the trial of the leaders of the Nazi party—or what was left of them. People often get the two movies mixed up.

Daniel: I'd like to see them again when I get back home. But I tell you what, I sure lost track of all the suicides. Every way you turned, somebody was taking his life!

Erik: It went with the obsession with power. Don't give the enemy the privilege of humiliating you. I wonder if we can park here and get into the courtroom? You go on. You have that tourist's look that just might incline them to let you in. Just shrug if the doorman asks you what you want. But whatever you do, don't clown around with that Nazi salute or you'll be the guest of the state, and then I'll say I don't know you.

Daniel: You just took the lighter side out of it.

Erik: There is no lighter side here. Germans are a people of laws and rules. You go on, and I'll find a parking spot.

Daniel: Where have you been? I have something to show you! Hurry! Hurry before someone stops us!

Erik: I couldn't park just anywhere, you know. The man in the uniform—

Daniel: Forget the man in the uniform. Come on, follow me! Quick!

Erik: I can't believe we're in this building.

Daniel: You haven't seen anything yet… Erik, we can look at those pictures later… Yes, I know they're of the trial here after the war. Just come on.

Erik: Do you ever wish you could just plug in to one of the walls and listen to the voices of the past?

Daniel: Sometimes I wish, yes, and at other times I— Go on in, there's nobody in there.

Erik: I don't believe it! This is it…this is the very room! Wow! Do you think we're allowed in here?

Daniel: Yes, the clerk at the door said it was okay. Let's not ask again or one of your "uniformed men in the land of laws" might decide otherwise.

Erik: What silence haunts this room, Daniel. But there was a day when the screams of the murdered were heard in here through the voices of—I'm still not sure we're supposed to be here without somebody in authority.

Daniel: Let's sit down, Erik. I must admit I never expected to get in here. Let's just pretend we're here by authority.

Erik: I don't like that word, *pretend*. Isn't that the way it all got started and ended? The whole thing was a charade—the pomp, the ceremony, the goose-stepping, the salute—but the incredible cost was very real.

Daniel: It's hard to put it all together. That one man could have such power to sway and destroy. I lost my relatives, you know—my uncle and my grandmother.

Erik: So did I. Let's just get our hearts to slow down a bit. I don't want to lose the moment. There are quite a few symbols and artwork here. Do you see what's above the door we entered? That is so fascinating!

Daniel: It's the serpent tempting Eve in the Garden, from the Book of Genesis.

Erik: Most visitors would wonder what that has to do with a courtroom.

Daniel: It has everything to do with it. Just everything. What an amazing reminder! Yes, the tempter told Adam and Eve that if they ate of a certain fruit they would be as God, discerning good and evil.

Erik: Talk about a chilling appropriateness. You know, I belong to the church, but for a long time I knew very little about the Bible. The state church here just takes true spirituality out of us. Still, there were some ministers who did try to stand in Hitler's way and even to assassinate him. Every German knows the name of Dietrich Bonhoeffer. Hitler finally executed him in Flossenberg.

Daniel: Now that's another thing, isn't it? Church and state… Hey, look high above the judge's chair. Those look like the tablets of stone with the Ten Commandments etched on them.

Erik: That's odd, though. It looks to me like there are only three commandments on the first tablet and seven on the second. Is that the way it's normally written?

Daniel: I may be wrong, but I think it's because the first three deal with our relationship to God and the last seven with our relationship to our fellow human beings. Without the first, there is no explaining the other. You talk about a land of laws! That's the law that stands supreme, above all other law. Isn't that what the prosecutor thundered when each defendant kept saying they were just following the law of their land?

Erik: I can hear it. "Gentlemen, is there not a law above our laws?" How profound, to have these in a courtroom in this way—the fall of humankind and the law that should govern our lives. That alone would make for a very interesting and profound discussion.

Daniel: Where's the building where the Nazi war criminals were held and executed? Wasn't it attached to the courthouse?

Erik: Yes, it's right behind us. It's connected to this building by an underground tunnel, and it's still used to house prisoners. They never quite see the bright sunshine once they come in.

Daniel: The scene in the movie of the executions was very sobering. One-by-one they had the rope placed around their necks, and then the floor just gave way from under them.

Erik: Literally and metaphorically. They had no ground to stand on, just the weight of their egos and their undisguised evil.

Daniel: I wonder what it would be like if Hitler were on trial in this courtroom and God were the judge?

Erik: Hitler wouldn't answer to anybody, not even to God. He didn't dialogue. His was a monologue. Dialogue involves reason, it requires a willingness to admit there's another opinion. To him, there was no other viewpoint but his.

Daniel: But that's because he tried to create his own reality. When he faced God, only God's reality would survive; all the sham and artificiality would collapse. Before God, Hitler is no different from the rest of us. Like a mask removed, our soul is laid bare when we stand before Him.

Erik: That would be quite a scene, wouldn't it? Hitler in the dock, Jesus the judge, Bonhoeffer the witness, the voices of the blood of millions crying out. I'd like to be able to witness that. Talk about the trial of the century. That would be the mother of all trials, if you ask me.

Daniel: The Lamb and the Führer…the ultimate reversal of metaphors on the way to finding the ultimate power.

Erik: You know, I had a friend who once said that if Hitler had asked Jesus for forgiveness at the end, all would have been forgiven. I find that—

Daniel: I've often thought of that, too. What would've happened if Hitler had fallen on his face and…that would be bizarre! What do you think Jesus would've said? I mean—

Erik: We don't have to go far to imagine someone asking for forgiveness. Did you ever read *The Sunflower* by Simon Wiesenthal? It's the true story of a Nazi officer begging Wiesenthal, a prisoner in a concentration camp, for forgiveness, and Wiesenthal just walks away, unable to grant the officer's plea. One wonders whether anyone could be so audacious as to grant forgiveness to someone like that.

Daniel: God can.

Erik: I could even write out a script for this. My friends and I used to talk about this. I was sort of the ringleader, asked to fill in the missing content in our imaginary scenarios.

Daniel: Well go ahead, then. I'm listening.

Erik: Okay, here goes. No, no, before I do that I would love to just think of his last hours in the bunker. From the network of underground rooms that enabled him to hide in secrecy to an open courtroom where nothing is hidden. From the bunker in Berlin to a judgment scene. Doesn't the Bible say it is appointed to man once to die and after that the judgment? A man who thought himself to be God, with a single, self-inflicted gunshot suddenly finds himself face-to-face with the real God, and every answer he gives to the questions he is asked must withstand the scrutiny of truth. I wonder if he even thought for a moment that he was headed straight to stand before God?

Daniel: Are you kidding? Remember what happened in that bunker in his final hours?

Erik: Well, the war was grinding the German machine to powder. The Allies were scoring one victory after another. Then the Soviet offensive began on January 16, 1945. Hitler gave his last speech on January 30, twelve years after his appointment as chancellor.

Daniel: He was trying to get back to the chancellery, wasn't he?

Erik: Yes, but it was already severely damaged by bombing, and the bunker was beneath the garden next to the chancellery.

Daniel: You know, my father used to say that Hitler's bunker was bigger than the homes of some world figures.

Erik: Yes, it was a network of rooms, you know, not some little hideaway. It had a large entry hall, a spiral staircase and all that. Plus, twelve rooms for his close confidants, rooms for orderlies, a doctor's office, a kitchen, and his own private quarters. He was moving between fits of rage and depression, in and out.

Daniel: One wonders if it was fear or confusion.

Erik: He was going for broke, digging deep into his persuasive powers. What else could he do? He called a handful of his aides together before heading to the bunker…

Hitler's secretary (reading memo from Albert Speer)**:** "The war is lost, Herr Führer. We are being routed on every front. Thousands of young Germans are dying. Time is against us. We have no resources left to—"

Hitler: Stop! Don't bring me such messages of doom! From total defeat springs the seed of the new. A desperate fight retains its eternal value as an example. We are the supreme race. No inferior nation is going to teach us a lesson. I must return to the bunker. Immediately! I shall live there till we have done the job. Make sure that Goebbels, Bormann, and my physician are there.

Secretary: The chancellery is badly battered, my Führer. One wing has been demolished by bombs.

Hitler: I don't care! Do not judge the big picture by the small scene. Get me back there immediately! My problem is that I have been too kind all along. I rue the day I decided to be so kind. Slaughter, destruction...that is what true victory is made of. We will show these idiots what we are made of. Their armies will lie buried beneath German dust. Millions of them.

Secretary: The reports are coming in that the people are terrified of Russian revenge. The word *surrender* is on many lips and—

Hitler: Do you not hear me? However grave the crisis, in the end it will be mastered by our unconquerable will. We will overcome this emergency. Never in my life will I accept surrender. I will fight on. We must stop these evil people and their evil leaders. Never give up. *Never!*

Secretary: Herr Speer would like a reply from you to his memo. There is more to it than I have read you.

Hitler: What does that traitor have to say?

Secretary: "My Führer, I am sending this memo to you to make sure I understand what you are saying. You wish everything destroyed—all electric plants, all our support systems, all our institutions? You want us to raze Germany to the ground?"

Hitler: You heard what I said. Tell him! The future belongs to the strong. I do not want the Eastern nations inheriting our strength. Burn everything. Everything! Give them nothing!

Daniel: Hold on a minute, Erik. I want this to reflect what really happened. Did Speer actually try to stop Hitler's scorched earth policy?

Erik: Yes, he did. He knew the game was over. Yet it was Speer who only a few years before had designed and planned the spectacular Party Rally that took place in this very city, not far from where we're standing right now. But in the end, he tried to stop it. He even tried to put poison gas into the bunker's air system, but it had just been reconfigured and that plot to kill Hitler failed, as well. Do you know there were forty-two attempts made to kill him…and all failed!

Daniel: I knew there had been several. But now there was an army closing in. He had to have seen the handwriting on the wall. The Russians were at the gates of Berlin, Erik. The city was being put to the torch. He was writing his will. What was this nonsense about looking at the plans to redesign Linz, the city of his youth, at the same time? He was planning a dream city to be rebuilt there. This man was a cauldron of contradictions!

Erik: How does one get into the mind of a man so singularly barbaric and at the same time so persuasive to the masses? That will always remain a mystery. Who were these who followed him? How were they so seduced? Doesn't make sense.

Hitler: Who would have thought that I'd be hiding here like an animal underground? I'd rather be a dead Achilles than a living dog! And after thirty years of giving myself, my life, my everything for the love of the Fatherland… Bring me the plans for Linz! I had a dream to rebuild it. It can still be done!

Eva Braun: But the Red Army is at the gates of Berlin, my Führer. Potsdam, Wurzburg, Dresden are all leveled to the ground. One eyewitness just sent word saying they resemble a moonscape. Is this the time to be looking at the plans for rebuilding Linz?

Hitler: Bring me the plans now! We will not be humiliated like this. Those foolish generals have cost me this. I made some mistakes. I should have begun the war earlier. That alliance with Italy was stupid.

SS Guard Commander Johann Rattenhuber: My Führer, the Soviet troops now occupy Tiergarten, Potsdamer Platz, and even the subway on Voltastrasse. They are in view of the chancellery.

Hitler: Leave me alone! I need to write some thoughts down. Don't disturb me till I'm finished. Nobody can shake my will. It was my will that brought us this far. Now my last will must be expressed. I will write it. If it is followed, the hope for the Fatherland will still be alive.

MY FINAL POLITICAL TESTAMENT
ADOLF HITLER, BERLIN, APRIL 29, 1945

Since 1914 when, as a volunteer, I made my modest contribution in the World War which was forced upon the Reich, over thirty years have passed.

In these three decades, only love for my people and loyalty to my people have guided me in all my thoughts, actions, and life. They gave me the strength to make the most difficult decisions, such as no mortal has yet had to face. I have exhausted my time, my working energy, and my health in these three decades.

It is untrue that I or anybody else in Germany wanted war in 1939. It was desired and instigated exclusively by those international statesmen who were either of Jewish origin or working for Jewish interests.... Centuries may pass, but out of the ruins of our cities and monuments of art there will arise anew the hatred for the people who alone are ultimately responsible: International Jewry and its helpers!...

But I left no doubt about the fact that if the peoples of Europe were again only regarded as so many packages of stock shares by these international money and finance conspirators, then that race, too, which is the truly guilty party in this murderous struggle would also have to be held to account: the Jews! I further left no doubt that this time we would not permit millions of European children of Aryan descent to die of hunger, nor millions of grown-up men to suffer death, nor hundreds of thousands of women and children to be burned and bombed to death in their cities, without the truly guilty party having to atone for its guilt, even if through more humane means.

After six years of struggle, which in spite of all reverses will go down in history as the most glorious and most courageous manifestation of a people's will to live, I cannot separate myself from the city which is the capital of this Reich. Because our forces are too few to permit any further resistance against the enemy's assaults, and because individual resistance is rendered valueless by blinded and characterless scoundrels, I desire to share the fate that millions of others have taken upon themselves, in that I shall remain in this city. Furthermore, I do not want to fall into the hands of enemies who for the delectation of the hate-riddled masses require a new spectacle promoted by the Jews.

I have therefore resolved to remain in Berlin and there to choose death of my own will at the very moment when, as I believe, the seat of the Führer and Chancellor can no longer be defended.

I die with a joyful heart in the awareness of the immeasurable deeds and achievements of our soldiers at the front, of our women at home, the achievements of our peasants and workers, and the contribution, unique in history, of our youth, which bears my name....

Many very brave men and women have resolved to link their lives to mine to the very end. I have requested them, and finally ordered them, not to do so, but instead to take part in the continuing struggle of the nation. I ask the commanders of the army, navy, and air force to strengthen by all possible means the spirit of resistance of our soldiers in the spirit of National Socialism, emphasizing especially that I too, as founder and creator of this movement, have preferred death to cowardly flight or even capitulation.

May it be one day a part of the code of honor, as it is already in the navy, that the surrender of an area or of a town is impossible, and above all in this respect the leaders should give a shining example of faithful devotion to duty unto death.

Before my death I expel the former Reichsmarschall Hermann Göring and deprive him of all the rights he may enjoy by virtue of the decree of June 29, 1941, and also by virtue of my statement in the Reichstag on September 1, 1939. I appoint in his place Grossadmiral Doenitz as President of the Reich and Supreme Commander of the Armed Forces....

Göring and Himmler, by their secret negotiations with the enemy, without my knowledge or approval, and by their illegal attempts to seize power in the state, quite apart from their treachery to my person, have brought irreparable shame to the country and the whole people....

Several men such as Martin Bormann, Dr. Goebbels, etc., together with their wives, have joined me by their own free will and do not wish to leave the capital of the Reich under any circumstances, but on the contrary are willing to perish with me here. Yet I must ask them to obey my request, and in this instance place the interests of the nation above their own feelings.

Through their work and loyalty they will remain just as close to me as companions after my death, just as I hope that my spirit will remain amongst them and will always accompany them.... I demand of all Germans, all National Socialists, men and women and all soldiers of the Armed Forces, that they remain faithful and obedient to the new government and to their President unto death.

Above all, I charge the leadership of the nation and their followers with the strict observance of the racial laws

and with merciless resistance against the universal poison-
ers of all peoples, international Jewry.

Given at Berlin, 29 April 1945, 4:00 AM.

ADOLF HITLER

As witnesses:

> Dr. JOSEPH GOEBBELS
> WILHELM BURGDORF
> MARTIN BORMANN
> HANS KREBS [1]

Daniel: That's just part of it, isn't it?

Erik: Yes. Then something interesting happened.

Hitler: During the years I did not think I could responsibly under-
take marriage. But now I have decided to take as my wife one so
faithful and loyal as Eva. At her request, she is joining me in death.
Death will compensate us. We choose death to escape the disgrace
of surrender. I want Goebbels and Bormann as the witnesses. Call
the magistrate Walter Wagner to perform this solemn ceremony.
We must abide by the law, you know. Now let us go and celebrate.

Bring in two hundred liters of gasoline. Where is that poison?
Call Sergeant Tornow.

Tornow: Yes, Führer, what may I do for you?

Hitler: Poison my dog Blondi as I leave the room. I want to make sure the poison works.

Tornow (to Professor Werner Haase of the medical staff)**:** You will need to bring some forceps, sir. They sense danger, you know. I will hold her down.

Haase: I'll pry open her mouth and force the poison down her throat. Be prepared for a struggle and then a convulsion... There, it's done. Call in the Führer.

Hitler: You all may leave now. Bring in the others from their bunkers. I will shake hands and bid them goodbye—Goebbels, Bormann, General Burgdorf, General Krebs, Frau Christian, Frau Junge, and my orderlies. Now we must part. You may all leave the room. Eva and I will remain here. You'll know when to come in.

[A few minutes go by...]

Goebbels: I have heard only one shot. Shouldn't we wait for the other?

Borman: There's been enough time. Maybe only one is going to do it. Let's go in.

What a picture of tragedy this is...our Führer's face smeared with blood. Eva looks like she decided only to poison herself. Her gun is unfired, still in her lap.

Rattenhuber: Russian shells are landing on the property. Let's wait a moment before we take the bodies outside to dispose of them."

Otto Günsche (Hitler's adjutant)**:** The bodies can be taken out now…follow me… Attention! Salute! Pour the gasoline over the bodies and toss those burning rags onto them… It's all over.

Hitler: What am I doing here? I thought I had ended everything. How can I still be alive? I never expected to see You! You of all people!

This is not the end I sought. That gunshot was to bring silence, not judgment. Where is the justice in all this? By what law will we function here? Who gives the orders? Why did You deceive me by not showing Yourself to me?

Jesus: If I did not show Myself to you, how do you know who I am?

Hitler: I can see the wounds in Your hands, and they are not saluting me. I did go to church on rare occasions. You are the Christ, are You not?

Jesus: Yes, Adolf. You are now in a different kingdom, made possible by My raising My arms in humiliation, not in mock ceremony.

Hitler: As I said, I never expected to see You. Where are You taking me? Why is everyone staring at me here? Do they also know me?

But I'm not in my uniform. I need my uniform. Don't take me like this! I order You! Is there no law and order here? Don't make light of me, I warn You!

Jesus: Nobody makes light of the sacred here. You will be tried by the best law and sentenced by the greatest grace ever offered. Where I dwell, hypocrisy and illusion are impossible. These people here are truly free. They have no fear. There is only one whom they fall prostrate before, and that is the living God.

Hitler: I know Him. I used His name. Yes…God is in control, isn't He? Not for a moment can I be accused of forgetting Him. Providence gave me my power. Some of my soldiers still wear buckles on their belts from the First World War that read "God is with us."

Jesus: There is nothing so dangerous as he who has ears but does not hear. And in a strange way you are half right. The heart of the king is in the hands of the Lord. The kings of the earth would never be in power but that My Father allows them that power. But before we go any further, Adolf, let Me tell you how fair your trial will be. You are now at the ultimate Court of Justice. You will be heard. You will be able to say anything you wish. Just remember that you did not give that chance to those who came to you for justice.

Hitler: Life forgives no weakness. It is the weak who bring hell, not the strong.

Jesus: Not so. I came for the weak of this world and will humble the strong. It is the sick who seek a physician, not those who think

The kings of the earth would

never be in power but that

my Father allows them

that power.

—Jesus

they are healthy. Your definition of strength and weakness is upside down.

Hitler: What do You know about real strength? You were spat upon, humiliated, scourged, beaten by the filth that fill this world. You talk to me about strength?

Jesus: Power does not lie in using it, but in having it and using it in the right way and for the right purpose. God does not take delight in the strength of a horse or in the strength of the legs of a man but in those that fear Him. You are so mistaken about power and authority. You wanted to gain the whole world, and all you have ended up doing is losing your soul!

Hitler: I nearly conquered the world *and* the souls of men! I mesmerized the crowds. I held them in the palm of my hand! Can You see it, even now? "Heil! Heil!" the chorus sounded. They wanted me. *Me!* They worshiped me! They feared me!

Jesus: One of those who knew you best described you as the coarsest, cruelest conqueror the world has ever known.

Hitler: Envy does not require genius.

Jesus: "Even now I cannot define or explain the power he held over them." Your words lacked the human note, the spiritual quality of a cultivated man. In your library you had no classic work, no single book on which the human spirit left its trace.

Hitler: How is it that even *You* cannot define where my power came from?

Jesus: Ah, so you *are* listening! I can define it, but those were not My words, Adolf. They were the exact words of your secretary, and she knew you well. Your books, your words, your dreams, your hate were all born out of the crushing of the soul. You never cared for people, any people. No, it was not just one race that you killed at will. You despised anyone who stood in your way. You said Jews, gypsies, and the handicapped were lesser than you. But they were not. You are the one who lowered yourself to realms of evil and wickedness that the world will remember with grief to the end of time. Professing yourself to be wise you became a fool. You cared more for the animal world than you ever did for the pinnacle of My creation—men and women made in the image of God!

Hitler: We Aryans are the Promethean bearers of light, kindling anew the fire of knowledge, climbing the path to mastery over all other beings of the earth. But the Jews are the vermin of civilization! The seducers of people! The refuse of all mankind!

Jesus: Why?

Hitler: Why? You ask why?

Jesus: Yes.

Hitler: They are the Bolsheviks of the earth. Moses was the first Bolshevik. Paul invented Christianity to destroy Rome. The Jews are the masterminds and power-greedy arch-foes. Behind and in the way of all human progress stands this Eternal Jew! Your own book says that they plundered the Egyptians. They are to blame for everything!

Jesus: Are you saying that they, the inferior ones, actually did better in plunder and profit than you, from a superior race?

Hitler: Don't You dare put words into my mouth!

Jesus: That is the first time you even thought that possible. You ordered and people listened. You came into a room and people stood to their feet. Now you accuse Me of putting words into your mouth? Do not your own words stand against you?

Hitler: No. I stand by my words. They could never stand against me.

Jesus: All right, let Me understand this. When you succeeded, whether by fraud or by brute power, you ascribed your success to providence. When the Jews succeeded and gained the upper hand, you attributed it to seduction. Can you explain this duplicity for Me?

Hitler: I tried to destroy them on that *Kristallnacht* when they fled like sheep from the slaughter…when their businesses were ravaged. I tried to rid the earth of them. My final solution almost succeeded. I was so close, but I failed. I failed! Now I stand before one who came as a dirty Jew and thinks He can pass judgment on me!

Jesus: Adolf, there is so much you don't understand. The destruction you caused among the nations of the world reflects the destruction you brought about within yourself. You see, a human being is not defined by his race. One's ethnicity is a sacred gift.

You say Paul invented Christianity. No, any attempt to destroy My message is an invention. Paul was inspired by My Holy Spirit when he told the Athenian philosophers that the God who made the world and everything in it made from one man every nation of men. And He determined the times set for them and the exact places where they should live. God did this so that men would seek Him and perhaps reach out for Him and find Him, though He is not far from each one.

Hitler: How can You possibly say that all races are equal? Our scientists proved that we are not equal. What about this herd mentality of some of the enslaved races? They are not equal to the noble Aryan.

Jesus: When you watched the "inferior" win out over the "superior," you couldn't handle it, could you? The truth was too offensive to your prejudice!

Hitler: Ah! What is Truth?

Jesus: Long before you someone else asked Me that but did not wait for an answer. You lived by what is natural but forgot that there is also the supernatural. You lived only with the horizontal dimension before you and forgot that there is also a vertical dimension. You lived a profane life and forgot that there is a sacred side to life. Life is a precious gift and it comes equally to all. Some religious people despise the irreligious and the other way around. The Romans despised the non-Roman; the Greeks thought themselves superior to all others. Have you ever wondered why, when I entered history, I came to the smallest and least recognized people at that time in history? The Jews were mocked by Greece, bullied by Rome, and enslaved by Babylon. I called them the apple of My eye, though they were nothing in humanity's grand schemes, because I chose them to reveal My message to all humankind. By choosing the weakest of all the peoples of the earth, I reminded the powers of the world that God's delight is not in human accomplishment, not in kingdoms or power, but in poverty of spirit.

Hitler: But those same Jews You chose rejected You. Why do You speak for them? They killed You!

Jesus: No, they didn't! First, no one could have taken My life if I had not willingly laid it down. Also, this is a fraudulent charge that is repeatedly reinvented. They alone did not kill Me— Romans, Greeks, people from everywhere in the world were gathered in Jerusalem on that day and participated in the events that took place. All of humanity must bear the blame for what happened.

But let Me ask you, why did you kill millions in the concentration camps? Why did you eliminate thousands of your own people who did not cooperate with you?

Hitler: You're not going to blame me for the killings carried out by others in the regime, are You?

Jesus: I thought you just blamed all the Jews for killing Me?

By choosing the weakest of
all the peoples of the earth,
I reminded the powers of
the world that God's
delight is not in human
accomplishment, not in
kingdoms or power, but in
poverty of spirit.

—Jesus

Hitler: What about the Jewish authorities? Why didn't they...this is no use. I'm confused. I need time to think.

Jesus: I gave you time, many times over. And every time your life was spared, you did even more evil. You couldn't see that killing and destruction are not what life is about. The heart of the king is in My hand. Yes, in My sovereign will I allow kings to come and go. Offenses must come, but woe to him through whom they come! Humanity does not know which way to turn unless there is someone with a vision to lead them in the way of truth and justice.

Hitler: Now You're talking! That's the vision I had, a Reich that would last a thousand years! I wanted to build a nation that would value work and discipline and be the super race that would set the standard for the rest of the world. I wanted to make sure they had the space they needed to develop as a people, to excel in all kinds of science and architecture. I wanted—

Jesus: Do you not know? Have you not heard? He who sits enthroned above the circle of the earth brings princes to naught and reduces the rulers of this world to nothing. The nations are like a drop in a bucket; they are regarded as dust on the scales. I weigh the islands as though they were fine dust. Believe Me, before Me all the nations are as nothing; I regard them as worthless and less than nothing. It is the Lord who is everlasting. He gives strength to the weary and increases the power of the weak. You tried to inspire the youth. You forgot that even the youth grow weary and young men stumble and fall. Only those who hope in Me, those who depend on Me, will renew their strength.

Come here with Me. Come, look at this cemetery in Normandy! Your young German men lie buried here. Look at their gravestones: eighteen years old, seventeen years old, this one is only fifteen! They were each somebody's son, somebody's brother. You promised them a Reich that would last a thousand years. Because of you and your dreams, they were cut short in the blossom of their youth. Now the very thing you so despised, My cross, is all that is left to mark their graves.

Come further…come over here, outside this concentration camp of Mauthausen. Here, where you tortured thousands, making them carry huge stones up these steep 186 stairs. Here, where so many died tortured deaths, stripped of their dignity as human beings. Read these words, Adolf. Read these words written to you: "O Germany, a blight on your mother! What have you done to your children?" And over here, "The voice of your brother's blood cries out from the ground."

Hitler: It was so reachable. I wanted to cover the shame of the past, the shame of the Versailles Treaty that was designed to humiliate us. The world turned against me first. I will not bend my knee. Oh, I wish I could do it all over again. I would—

Jesus: No, Adolf. That is only part of the story. You lied to those you killed as you lied about yourself.

Hitler: Is this the end of the road for me?

Jesus: Not yet. First, you must hear what the world needs to hear about who you really were. There is nothing done in secret that will not be revealed openly. No cover of pomp and ceremony will mask the hideous evil of any life. This is where you really begin, when you think you are at the end. Time ticks away moments. Eternity brings to focus all that time tried to cover.

Welcome to the Court of Eternal Justice, Adolf. Unlike your court, where you did not allow the defendants to speak, you may do so. Unlike your court, where trumped-up charges were designed to accomplish your agenda, only truth survives here. Unlike your court, where blame can be passed from one to the other, here in the end each person sees himself or herself before the supreme Judge of all the earth who will do right. Enter and be seated. No oath is needed here because the moment a lie is spoken, it will burn away into smoke. Only what is true will survive.

Hitler: I can't see the face of the judge. Who is it?

Jesus: You do not need to see Him. You will hear His voice. You will see other faces though, faces you will recognize. Are you ready, Adolf?

Hitler: If You will give me the same power of speech I had on earth, I am ready to face anyone. They will not be able to stand before me and dare to question or accuse me!

Jesus: You have it, Adolf. Speak.

Hitler: What are the charges that anyone dares to bring against me?

Jesus: What charges did you bring against those you exterminated?

Hitler: I ordered the final solution only to rid the earth of those who plundered and destroyed superior races and cultures.

Jesus: Any other charges?

Hitler: Those who were traitors to my desires and decrees, who refused to cooperate with the Reich I was forming or stood in my way.

Jesus: That by which you judged, you shall be judged. Where did you spend your youth?

Hitler: In beautiful Linz, in Austria.

Jesus: Do you remember seeing the huge sculpture in the center of that square?

Hitler: The one dedicated to Charlemagne and the Holy Roman Empire?

Jesus: Yes. What are the words written there?

Hitler: Let me think…something about God being one in essence, three in person, holy, strong, immortal.

Jesus: Anything else?

Hitler: It said something about freedom and service to Him alone. But that was the Holy Roman Empire. You know how Napoleon changed *that* precedent. When the head of the church was going to crown him, he grabbed the crown and put it on his own head.

He did not want to be associated with any submission to anything divine, even symbolically. He broke from every connection with divine appointment. And that is the way I saw myself. I did not need to take direction from any divine being.

Jesus: That was the turning point in your thinking. You made yourself above My law. You thought yourself above God.

Hitler: I was not going to allow the church to influence my people!

Jesus: I never commissioned the church to rule over governments. On two occasions My disciples wanted to crown Me king. But I told them that My kingdom was not of this world and that My servants would be leading no armed rebellion in My behalf or at My bidding. You do not understand how to rule people. You will never win a person's heart with the sword. But your own heart did not understand that, Adolf.

Hitler: What is *he* doing here? I…I recognize—

Jesus: He is the first witness to speak to your self-glory.

Hitler: But this is Speer! Why, you traitor…

Jesus: No need to fill the room with smoke, Adolf! Let him speak.

Speer: Yes, it's true. I came under his spell.

Jesus: To what do you attribute that?

Speer: At first it was just that I was an architect, with plans and ambition for my career, and he was an admirer of my skill. But it wasn't long before the admiration moved from him admiring me to me admiring him.

Jesus: Keep talking and your own mouth will convict you, Albert.

Speer: From the first time I heard him, I was in awe. At first, the rallies were small. I remember one occasion in the early days at the Krone Circus in Munich. The auditorium was filled an hour and a half before he came. There was excitement, a buzz, an air of solemnity and revelry at the same time, an air of anticipation…like a god was coming. The blood red and black of the swastikas that were everywhere was almost hypnotizing. And when word spread that he was in the building…I remember the song that was sung:

> We are the hungry toilers
> A strong courageous band
> We grip our rifles firmly
> In sooty calloused hands.

> The storm troops stand at ready
> The racial fight to lead
> Until the Jews are bleeding
> We know we are not freed.

Now as I look back…at how the crowds—

Hitler: How the crowds what?

Jesus: Please let him finish.

Speer: His way with words—steeped in emotion, augmented by ceremony, exaggerated by hysterical crowds, driven home by screaming rhetoric. Why? When all seems lost, a new voice that claims the power to restore becomes one's only hope. As an architect I decided I would help him build his kingdom. The night I remember most was the night in Nuremberg…the Zeppelinfield Rally. I mean, it was the making of a god.

Hitler: That was a night I always remembered with intense satisfaction. What a night! Please tell how you did it, Speer. I want to enjoy it again.

Jesus: Go ahead, Albert. I want your own words to tell what really happened.

Speer: Hundreds of thousands of the party faithful had gathered from all around Germany. Hitler arrived close to eight p.m. The darkness was suddenly dispelled by a flood of white light from 150 projectors about forty feet apart, all around the field. In that black-grey sky their beams met to form a blazing crown over the whole area. It was regal and mesmerizing, an unforgettable sight. Thirty thousand banners streamed into the arena, their silver point tassels flashing in the light. It almost created the effect of a gothic cathedral in the sky. The…the…

Jesus: Why do you stop?

Hitler: Please don't stop now! Finish…finish what you are saying!

Speer: Can't You see it coming? Can't You see what happened, Jesus?

Jesus: I can and I could. What did you see, Albert?

Speer: I saw reality enshrouded in a farce. I became the seducer and the seduced. I made the scene, I created the aura, I used the power of light and sound and color to frame reality in a surreal masquerade. I made him look that night like the lie he had manufactured, seducing minds—including my own—to believe it was the truth. I wish I had had the courage then to call my own bluff. I weep now as both the deceiver and the deceived.

Jesus: That is how the human mind deceives itself.

Speer: Yes, at the end it was plain. This is the hell of the human heart when it realizes its own seductive powers. I should have known! But he promised that his was a kingdom to transcend all other kingdoms. We made our illusory world and then worshiped that illusion till, like a dumb idol, it was shattered before our eyes. Now the graves…

Hitler: I loved you, Speer. But traitors always run when their champion is down. You know that, don't You, Jesus? You had a traitor in Your midst as well.

Jesus: You have that same flaw that all in your position have. You see that we have one thing in common and conclude that we have everything in common.

Hitler: I'm under no illusion. I am well aware that Your kingdom and mine are very different.

Jesus: You'll find out that is true in more ways than you realize. Here is another voice.

Hitler: Ru…Rudolf Höss!

Jesus: Speak, Rudolf.

Höss: Ah, it's too late. But relive it, I must. He…he put me in charge of the camps that were to carry out his final solution. Yes, I exterminated thousands of human beings…millions. But I was not aware of the first gassing of humans; I remember much better the gassing of nine hundred Russians. They walked calmly into the gas chambers thinking they were going to be deloused there. The door was locked and the gas poured in through openings in the ceiling. I remember some screaming, "Gas!" And a great roar began and a rush to the doors. How long the killing took I do not know. The hum was heard for quite a while, however. After several hours we opened the door and aired out the room. That is when I saw gassed corpses for the first time… But I must be frank. This gassing had a calming effect on me, since the mass extermination of the Jews was to begin soon, and neither Eichmann nor I knew what method of killing might be used. We felt this was the most painless and noble.

Hitler: You scoundrel.

Höss: I was a family man. I went back to my wife and children every evening. I just did my job. This was what was asked of me and I did it.

Jesus: Did the screams not haunt you, thousands every day?

Höss: As someone has said, "One death is a tragedy, millions are just a statistic."

Jesus: Every time you killed one person, you attacked the very image of God that is present in every human being. The evil of the holocaust was that you chose to stab at the image of God in each of your victims.

Hitler: I never walked into a concentration camp!

Jesus: Did you not know what was happening? Were you not told what was going on?

Hitler: I set my sights on an end. The means no longer mattered.

Jesus: You have spoken the truth. Therein, you betray your own soul. You see, Adolf, when you as a young man were denied entrance to the Academy of Fine Arts, you chafed under that rejection. Do you remember that?

Hitler: As well as I remember anything. I was bitter and angry. Nobody had the right to reject me. Not just once, more than once.

Jesus: You were bitter that you were denied entrance to a school? You were in anguish over that? Did you not for a moment think of the rejection you placed upon millions of people because of their birth? Only their birth. Did you not think for a moment of the millions you were consigning to a grave just because of their race, or because they stood in your way to absolute power?

Hitler: People are like animals. They do not know which way to turn. They are interested only in having a full stomach. I wanted to make Germany the greatest force on earth so that the world would take note. Those who did not understand this vision needed to be obliterated.

Jesus: Here is one who you tried to obliterate. Speak, dear woman.

Woman: My name...my name is Sara Tuvel Bernstein.[2] Do I have to see his face?

Jesus: He needs to see yours.

Woman: I was a seamstress. Because I was a Jew I was arrested and taken to the concentration camp in Dachau. I was told I would be able to work and that would make me free. That's what the sign said at the gate: "Work makes free." I was deceived right from the start. I couldn't believe they were systematically, cruelly killing us. Each day, somebody else was missing. They starved us one day at a time. They deprived us of food and drink. Each day I wondered what was happening to my brain. I would go through periods of dizziness because of malnourishment.

Then, early one morning, I slipped out of my bed and went looking for worms to eat. That's what it had come to...worms to feel some warmth inside my body.

Hitler: Stop!

Jesus: She will finish.

Woman: I remember that as I was bent down poring over the grass, I suddenly felt eyes staring at me from the other side of a window. I was scared because it was a horrific face, like a phantom head stuck on top of a pole. I caught my breath, and my heart started racing. I approached the window to see who this was, and like a wave coming over me, it dawned on me. The ghost was me! I was looking at my own reflection! That's when I knew I had all but lost my person in the torture chambers of Dachau.

Hitler: Don't try to arouse my pity. She would have been better off gassed instead of prolonging her suffering.

Jesus: Because she was Jewish, is that right?

Hitler: How often do You want me to say it? Yes!

Jesus: Here, meet this man, Adolf.

Hitler: I don't know who he is.

Jesus: He's not Jewish. He's one of your own. He's only seventeen.

Helmut Altner:[3] I was on the road to Berlin. We were hours away from being crushed by the oncoming Russian army. On the desolate street at night I see two SA men in uniform standing by a lamppost. I lift my eyes and see a civilian hanging from that post. There is a red cord around his neck that has bitten deeply into his flesh. His face is blue, his eyes are sunken into his sockets. Around his neck hangs a sign, written in shaky letters: "I am Otto Meyer. I was too cowardly to fight for my wife and child. That is why I am hanging here like a rat."

Hitler: Why is he complaining about another man's fate? What's it to him?

Altner: That was the fate even to the end of those who refused to join in your carnage. They were not just killed, they were held up for all to see the "shame" of refusing to submit to the Führer's power. Such is the method of demagogues. They terrorize you and your family and shame you into atrocities, and then they say they don't recognize you!

Jesus: There is one more you will hear from. You will recognize him.

Hitler: Why do I have to listen to so many?

Jesus: They are nowhere near the number who want to face you and make you hear what they have to say. Meet the man you hanged at Flossenberg.

Hitler: Oh, he's one of those in the July 20 group. What losers they were! Claus Schenk Graf von Stauffenberg and his band of murderers tried to assassinate me. There was a clear reason here for me to retaliate. What would You expect me to do? That very night I had Stauffenberg shot. My justice was swift and uncompromising. Yes, one hundred of them were wiped out by my order. I had

48   RAVI ZACHARIAS

The light that shines from

everyone who knows

Me comes from within.

There is no need for

artificial adornment.

—Jesus

the Gestapo follow up on the rest, and this deceiver was among them. He's supposed to be a pastor and he tried to become a killer. Why is he in such a privileged position here? He looks different from the way I remember him. Then, he was just another human being. Now he seems to be at perfect peace and his expression radiates a light.

Jesus: The light that shines from everyone who knows Me comes from within. There is no need for artificial adornment. But he was already in prison when that attempt to kill you was made on July 20.

Hitler: I needed to get anybody I thought would have knowledge of it. I reacted with immediacy.

Jesus: So justice was swift and ruthless? You get a fairer trial here. You actually get a chance to speak. Your own words might convict you though, so be warned. I will let him speak.

Dietrich Bonhoeffer: So, Herr Hitler, we finally meet face-to-face. I knew this day would come.

Hitler: You knew, did you? You could not accomplish even one killing. How could you know!

Bonhoeffer: You can shout all you want. I did not fear you then, even less now. There is a marker now where you hanged me. It reads, "For God did not give us a spirit of timidity, but a spirit of power, of love and of self-discipline." No, we were not intimidated by the charade of your persona. We saw through you. We knew the evil that lurked inside you. From being a Führer to standing in front of a judge is a long way down, isn't it?

Hitler: What makes you think I fear you?

Bonhoeffer: You make the same mistake now. Have you seen what is prepared for those who reject the love of God and how you will now spend the rest of eternity?

Hitler: I will get my turn to make my case, won't I?

Jesus: Yes, you will. But Bonhoeffer is not finished yet.

Hitler: Have you ever wondered why, if you were on God's side in this matter, your stupid plan to kill me didn't work? Imagine that coward Stauffenberg! He places the device in his briefcase, pushes it toward me, and leaves the room, supposedly to go to the toilet. Kaboom! A few minutes later and he is celebrating, not knowing that someone moved the briefcase unwittingly, and that I was spared. How did your God come through for you then?

Bonhoeffer: You ask how, if I was serving God, the plan didn't work and He spared you?

Hitler: Exactly!

Bonhoeffer: Let me tell you a little story. It was a cold night in December, 1931. A European politician had finished his lecture tour in New York and had left the famed Waldorf-Astoria Hotel to visit a friend. As he crossed the street, he forgot to look in the right direction for traffic. Suddenly, thud! He was hit by a car and thrown like a puppet into midair. In his words, "I do not understand why I was not broken like an eggshell or squashed like a gooseberry."

Hitler: What sort of story is that? How does it have anything to do with what we're talking about?

Bonhoeffer: Do you know who that was?

Hitler: Am I supposed to know? Of course I don't!

Bonhoeffer: Are you interested to know who it was?

Hitler: I have no time for games.

Bonhoeffer: It was Winston Churchill. He should have been pulverized on the streets of New York in 1931.

Hitler: Scum! If only providence had given the aging and senile England another Pitt instead of this Jew-besotted, half-American drunkard, Germany could have led this world with a free hand and England could have been spared six years of war!

Bonhoeffer: I only share that since you think you were spared by providence to do what you wanted to do. What makes you think you weren't anticipated and that a nemesis wasn't raised up to stop you? God works in His own ways and times, you know. He didn't have to stop you in our way. He stopped you His way and allowed all to see what a world without God looks like.

Jesus: Adolf, I do not have to violate human freedom in order to bring My plan into effect. The lot is cast into the lap, but every

God works in His own ways
and times, you know.
He didn't have to stop you
in our way. He stopped you
His way and allowed all to
see what a world without
God looks like.

—Dietrich Bonhoeffer

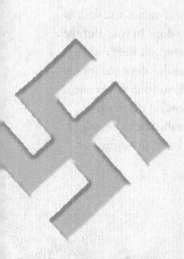

decision is from the Lord. With the righteous, I show Myself righteous. With the shrewd, I will show Myself shrewd.

Bonhoeffer: There is something you forget about God's sovereign ways, Herr Hitler. You think you can move human history by your own power and schemes. You cannot accelerate the march of history by one moment. God has a plan all His own.

Hitler: I left my mark on history and that's what counts.

Jesus: Everyone leaves his or her mark. On what basis do you think you should be judged?

Bonhoeffer: May I answer that?

Hitler: He asked me, not you, and I'll answer Him. Judge me on the basis of my love for my country and the desire to see the humiliation of my people ended. The world hated us before I hated it. Did You read the treaty they made us sign? Did You see the millions who were jobless because our money was worthless? Was that not just cause to go to war and turn the tables on Europe?

Jesus: You say you resented a treaty that was unfair. You wish to be judged on the basis of what was unfairly done to you? But these people now presenting their cases against you, you were ruthless with them. What did they do to you? What did those millions of children you had gassed or shot to death do to you? When one of your henchmen was assassinated, you demanded the death of thousands in bloody reprisal. Would you really like to be judged on the same basis you judged others? The weak, the silent, the ones who were condemned just for being born the way they were? Or others, for refusing to join the hell you were creating. Was that fair? Who do you think you were to make those decisions?

Hitler: I was shaped by my time to lead a world that had gone astray.

Bonhoeffer: Jesus, I would like to answer him with what I wrote in my journal one day, if I may. I pondered this again and again. I was a pacifist. I did not want to take up arms for any cause. Then this mass murderer came onto the stage of history and I could no longer live without doing something to stop the killing. I did not seek to kill. *I wanted to stop the killing.* If there were some way to stop this man, the carnage could be stemmed.

Hitler: What do I care about who *you* were? What's that got to do with the question of who I thought *I* was?

Bonhoeffer: Everything! I wrestled with the purpose of life. I kept asking, Who am I? I knew that at the core of everyone's being this question has to be answered. Only then can everything else be explained. When you imprisoned me, I nearly lost it on one occasion, and then I penned these words. They became my constant reminder in all that I did:

> Who am I? They often tell me
> I would step from my cell's confinement
> calmly, cheerfully, firmly,
> like a squire from his country house....

Am I then really all that which other men tell of?
Or am I only what I know myself,
restless and longing and sick, like a bird in a cage,
struggling for breath, as though hands were compressing
   my throat,
yearning for colours, for flowers, for the voices
   of the birds,
thirsting for words of kindness, for neighbourliness,
trembling with anger at despotisms and petty
   humiliation,
tossing in expectation of great events,
powerlessly trembling for friends at an infinite distance,
weary and empty, at praying, at thinking, at making,
faint, and ready to say farewell to it all?…

Who am I? They mock me, these lonely questions
   of mine.
Whoever I am, thou knowest, O God, I am thine.[4]

Once I answered the question in those terms, life took on a whole new purpose. I belonged to this God who loved me and created me in His love and for His love.

Hitler: You see, even there my kindness allowed you to be able to write in prison and bring yourself some healing. But those thoughts you have expressed were not mine and have nothing to do with me.

Bonhoeffer: How you miss the point! Never mind. So you gave me the opportunity to shape my thoughts?

Hitler: Yes, of course.

Bonhoeffer: Yet you have the audacity to blame God for how you turned out because of the twists of history? We shape ourselves, Herr Hitler. We shape ourselves.

Jesus: Adolf, who you are is not what people say about you. It is not the uniform you wear. It is not all the accolades men and women shower upon you. It is not the screams of the adoring crowds. It is not all that you hear from your well-wishers. It is how you define yourself in relation to Me. That is what life is. You are either for Me or against Me. There is no middle ground.

I once asked My disciples two critical questions: First, who do men say that I am, and then, who do you say that I am? My mission was to do the will of My Father who is in heaven. My mission was all about My relationship with My Father.

Hitler: Well, *my* mission was to be who I was—the Führer of the Third Reich! I was born to rule the earth. When I spoke people listened. No, they trembled. I had what it took to lead the ignorant masses.

Bonhoeffer: As you killed, tortured, and conquered by force was there never a twinge of thought within you that maybe what you were doing was wrong?

Hitler: I am a man with an iron will. Nobody will break that.

Besides, what do you mean, wrong? How does one define wrong? You can't tell me I'm wrong. What is wrong? Must not each one define his or her ethic?

Bonhoeffer: I defined it on the basis of who Jesus is and what He said—to love the Lord my God with all my heart and my neighbor as myself—and that made all the difference in the world!

Hitler: If loving your neighbor was so important to you, why did you try to thwart me when I reached out to you Christians? I even sought God's blessing upon my leadership.

Bonhoeffer: You weren't the first one to claim that God was on your side. But claiming it and acting in keeping with His character are two different things. Jesus walked with the weak of this world— the sick, the lame, the blind. You called them weaklings, the refuse of society, and said they had to be done away with. He talked of humility; you talked of pride. He talked of submission; you talked of conquering. He talked of love; you talked of hate. He allowed even those who opposed Him to speak; you silenced even those who just wanted to ask questions. He allowed those who despised Him the freedom to make their choice. For you, the only freedom possible was to implement your plan for world domination.

Oh yes, in the beginning you made some kind of pledge to bring Christians onto your side. But that's not where you stopped. You then asked Christians to sign policies that despised others, that victimized some, that allowed only those of the Aryan race to be bishops. You even co-opted the pope and promised all kinds of breaks if the church would remain silent as you killed and tortured and destroyed.

Hitler: Only one power at a time can rule.

Bonhoeffer: But that power must not coerce either belief or disbelief in God. It bothered me no end that the power structure of the church was selling out to you in order to secure its own power and sacrificing the gospel at the altar of political expediency! That's when I left the mainline church to join the ranks of those who saw through you and your scheme to destroy human life for the sake of your own powerbase.

Hitler: There you have it from your own mouth! I knew I would trap you sooner or later! So you accuse me of killing, but you yourself had no hesitancy to kill. Jesus, how can he be one of Yours if he too violated the image of God by attempting to kill me?

Bonhoeffer: You can ask me that, Herr Hitler. I'll answer you! I told you that the first question I had to answer was, "Who am I?" I answered that I am a child of God. But there was a second question: "What law am I ultimately responsible to obey?"

Hitler: So you too answered to your own laws, then?

Bonhoeffer: Please let me finish. It's not that simple. In the story of Israel's conquest of the Promised Land, even a harlot knew to help the spies when they came. She knew that the land was full of bloodshed and injustice and that the ones she harbored sought to do justice, to love mercy, and to walk humbly before God. I am a child of God—that is the only way I could define myself—yet a child of God under the political system of a man willing to exterminate millions without any reason other than his own prejudice and ambition. That's why I joined the underground intelligence to have you removed!

Hitler: You served your ethic; I served mine.

Bonhoeffer: Don't get me distracted with the repetition of your arguments. I have waited for the day to speak my conscience on this because you denied me that right. You were no Führer…you were a Verführer, a misleader!

Hitler: Oh yes, I remember how you used that word in one of your sermons. I stopped that broadcast of yours before you had a chance to tell the nation. How funny that was to me. Here you were on the air, in the middle of your sermon, and we pulled the plug on you!

Bonhoeffer: Yes, and you prove that all-important point. I tried by the laws of the land to stop you. I tried to warn the people that we had a master of genocide in our midst, an imposter. But you silenced anyone who disagreed with you. I remember the day my brother-in-law, Hans, quoted a verse of Scripture to me from Matthew 26 that "all who draw the sword will die by the sword."

Hitler: And you surely did.

Bonhoeffer: Yes, I did, and that was the price I was willing to pay. It was a turning point for me. Are you listening to what I'm saying?

Hitler: I am listening. But I want to ask You, Jesus…if everything I say can be used against me, can I be forgiven if I choose to repent?

Jesus: You will have your answer in the most certain terms, Adolf. You have My word on that. Dietrich…

Bonhoeffer: The masquerade of evil was being played out. I had to choose whether to stand by or stand my ground. And who stands his ground? I watched. I pondered. It is not the rationalist. He thinks a small dose of reason will put the world aright. But soon he is disappointed with the irrationality of the world, and his bubble of reason bursts. It is not the moral purist. The power of evil traps him into nonessentials till everything becomes defined but with no power to act. Then there is the man of conscience. But even he in the end becomes content with a salved conscience rather than a clear one as evil deceives him as well. Duty then seems the other option. But duty finds conflicts with so many to whom he owes some allegiance and duty ends up giving the devil his due.

Hitler: Doesn't seem like you had any answers.

Bonhoeffer: I did. I do. Some seek refuge from the rough and tumble of public life in the sanctuary of their own virtue. Such men are compelled to seal their lips and shut their eyes to all the injustice around them. Only at the cost of self-deception can they keep themselves pure from the defilements of responsible action.

For all that they achieve, what they leave undone will still torment their peace of mind. They will either go to pieces in the face of this disquiet, or develop into the most hypocritical of all Pharisees.

The person who stands his or her ground is not the one whose ultimate criterion is his reason, his principles, his conscience, his freedom, or his virtue. The only person who stands his ground is the one who is ready to sacrifice all things when he is called to obedient and responsible action in faith and exclusive allegiance to God—not for land or goods or personal gain, but for the upholding of life in its sacred right to live and in its freedom to self-determination. That person seeks to make his whole life a response to the question and the call of God. I chose to be that kind of person.

I had to come to a decision. I did not believe killing is for man to do. But when I saw what was going on, I had to respond the only way I could. My decision to eliminate you was born not for any personal reasons. I didn't try to stop you even when you denied me the privilege of marrying the woman I loved. I didn't stop you when my family was in danger. I didn't stop you when you shut down my seminary or humiliated and persecuted my students or took my home. I continued to appeal to the conscience of the people to remove you from office. But you denied me even the opportunity to speak of the evils you were doing. When you silenced those who spoke out for the preservation of life, you crossed a line. That is not God's way; that is not the way of allowing us to be truly human. I did not try to kill those who were your instruments. I did not go and kill innocent people. I wanted you

The only person who stands
his ground is the one who is
ready to sacrifice all things
when he is called to obedient
and responsible action
in faith and exclusive
allegiance to God.
—Dietrich Bonhoeffer

removed because you were the one by whose word and order our law was stifled, changed, and abused in order to give you sole authority to kill. It was you I sought to remove, not anyone else. You took a series of steps, and then I took mine.

First, you took sole and complete authority over law. Then you took sole and complete authority for the extermination of life. Then you silenced anyone who questioned that authority.

You turned the courts into halls of human abuse. You set up a government that was an instrument of torture and pain. You denied humanity its essential racial worth. You denied people any freedom to believe or disbelieve in God. You enforced belief in you even over belief in God.

Did you really expect us to stand back and watch the masses burned, tortured, killed and do nothing? You wanted us as the church to support genocide?

Hitler: So to take my life was okay?

Bonhoeffer: By what moral law do you condemn the decision I made?

Hitler: Moral law? What's that?

Bonhoeffer: You see, on your own terms you lose the right to condemn me. You borrow from my sacred view of life to even legitimize your question. That's how morally bankrupt you became and made our nation.

Hitler: So my life was to be taken?

Bonhoeffer: I would have rather tried you in the courts, but you took control of the courts. I would have rather appealed to your moral reasoning, but you rejected moral reasoning. I would have rather tried you by the law of the land, but you abolished it and made yourself the supreme law. Any direction I looked for a solution, the answer became the taking of a life—either yours or standing back and letting the innocent continue to be killed. It was not so much that the choice was evil but that to leave the situation unchecked was evil. I sought the cross each day and wept for the courage to do what was right, for what would guard the absoluteness of the sacredness of life for all, and to be forgiven if I was wrong.

In the complexities of life you start with the sacredness of life, and as evil invades and powers seduce, there emerges a hierarchy of choices. I rested on God's power to raise the dead and on my willingness to protect human life as not merely a political ideology. It was the very reason nations have to sometimes choose to go to war—to stop the killing, not to become autonomous over all law.

The world was not coming to our rescue. The world looked on for too long as millions screamed in gas chambers. I could not look on any longer. No, I would not go on a rampage. It was you and you only that needed to be stopped. For myself, I was willing to die for that cause to save humanity. When you sent me to the gallows, I was not afraid. I had done what was right, the only thing I could do to save millions.

My colleague, Martin Niemöller, whom you imprisoned in Buchenwald for speaking against you, said these famous words: "They came first for the Communists, and I didn't speak up because I wasn't a Communist. Then they came for the Jews, and I didn't speak up because I wasn't a Jew. Then they came for the trade unionists, and I didn't speak up because I wasn't a trade unionist. Then they came for the Catholics, and I didn't speak up because I was a Protestant. Then they came for me, and by that time no one was left to speak up."

I spoke up because I valued life, and God's love is for all mankind, not just for the powerful. The character of God beckons us to love every man, woman, and child, even those who hate Him. Your character was hate and power, which hatched your evil scheme to control humanity.

Hitler: And I sent you to the gallows for that!

Bonhoeffer: I'm home now, Herr Hitler. You're an alien here, and your time and place was determined by your choice.

Jesus: Whoever has thought that the judgment day would not bring to light everything that has happened ought to listen in on this conversation. Adolf, you asked how one defines right and wrong. You asked the right question, but it is not the question you should have asked first. Your first question should have been, "How does one define life?" How one defines ethics is based on how one defines life itself.

Hitler: I never quite got down to that because for me the direction of history was primary. I had no time for anything that stood in the way of that.

Jesus: But you cannot write a story for mankind until you know what man is. I am Life. I created life in humanity. You are made in the image of God, made to conform to Me, the image of His Son. I am ultimate reality and everything to the contrary is spurious. I have no beginning and no end. You have a beginning but were made to live forever. I am uncreated and eternal. I created the pattern for which God fashioned your soul. You will remember the prophet Isaiah, because you quoted him often enough—"Unto us a child is born, unto us a Son is given."

Hitler: Yes, at Christmastime we often heard that when I was in school.

Jesus: Yes, but you never listened to it. Listen now. The child is born…the Son is given. Do you see the difference?

Hitler: No.

Jesus: The Son was not born. I am the Son and I eternally existed in relationship with My Father. Those were the words you read on the monument in Linz, but never ever pondered. You see, in My Word, the Bible, you will read that there is oneness in the very Godhead—the Father, Son, and Holy Spirit. God is a being in relationship. This is so unique and so true that it is the greatest mystery in all of faith.

Bonhoeffer: Isn't this the very truth Mohammed denied?

Jesus: Yes, he denied it, and his followers have never been taught the truth about it. Let Me ask you the same question, Adolf, that I have asked so many who have questioned Me. Do you know what has been the greatest search in philosophy to this day? Do you know what has been the greatest search in culture to this day? Do you know what has been the greatest struggle within the human heart to this day?

Hitler: Those are three questions, not one.

Jesus: You have spoken correctly, but the answer is the same to all three.

Hitler: I would say, then, that the greatest search is for self-understanding. And the answer is that some, like me, are superior in their self-understanding.

Jesus: I know what is in your heart. I am telling you now where you have failed and what is in God's heart. The greatest search in philosophy, culture, and in the human heart is for unity in diversity. With all that we see around us, how do we find harmony of the soul and harmony one with the other?

Bonhoeffer: The Greeks sought this, didn't they? And that's why the university was formed, to find unity in diversity. I remember when teaching in New York, seeing on every coin "E Pluribus Unum"—out of many, one—and often wishing that could be true for the whole world. Lord, how do You speak to this? My heart is eager.

The greatest search in

philosophy, culture,

and in the human heart is for

unity in diversity.

With all that we see around

us, how do we

find harmony of the soul

and harmony one

with the other?

—Jesus

Jesus: The Greeks stopped short of the means to the end. Yes, ancient cultures looked for the answer, and younger nations have also sought it. But they forgot the real problem. When you were framed in God's image, the purpose was clear: to bring you into perfect relationship with God so that you might perfectly reflect Him and in that perfection make the correct choices and respect the dignity of choice as well as the ramifications of choice. Harmony has to come from within, first. You see, the diversity inside each human being first has to be tamed. My apostle Paul referred to that when he wrote that he had certain propensities that left him divided, until he found unity with the salvation I offered and with My Spirit indwelling him. Unity and diversity can never be found outside until it is first found within.

Bonhoeffer: I get it! There was both unity and diversity in the Trinity, the first cause of all life, and until we find that communion with God, we can have no real unity within ourselves or with our fellow human beings.

Jesus: That's it. Every man and woman is at war within himself or herself. There is a gradual dying on the inside. With every choice that's made autonomously, the nature of sin is compounded until inside the person, death gradually takes over. Those who kill and destroy and plunder are only revealing the death and hell that is inside them. They want to kill, while I teach them that even to hate is wrong. They discuss how to deal with adultery; I try to help them to not even lust. All acts were first thoughts within.

They have no peace within, and because they are not at peace with themselves they are not at peace with the world and with their fellow man. Each of you were fashioned for a relationship, and you will keep on hungering for relationships until you find the blueprint of all relationships, the one God, who Himself is a being in relationship. I came to change the way the heart thinks so that it will change the way the mind acts.

Hitler: Relationships were never important to me.

Jesus: I want you to hear Me clearly, Adolf, because you have spoken the truth. I told you that God is a being in relationship, an inviolable relationship. Yet, there came a moment when I was sent by My Father to lay down My life on that cross that you so often saw. Do you know what that meant?

Hitler: Never could figure it out.

Jesus: Neither do so many. On that cross, what was eternally inviolable—My relationship with the Father—was violated by sin, and I cried out in My abandonment. If you read My psalmist, David, he tells you that My separation was to demonstrate what sin actually does. It breaks the relationship of what is the most sacred. You were a dead man to God on the inside so you attacked the image of God on the outside. You are right—you had no relationships because you rejected the one who created you for relationship. Instead, you became the destroyer of life.

Hitler: I lived for ownership, not relationship.

Jesus: Again, you were not alone in that. That is the condition of every human heart, Adolf. Everyone wishes to own—to own themselves, to own property, to own power, and to own their destiny.

Hitler: And what's wrong with that?

Jesus: You're not listening.

Bonhoeffer: He never did, and now that he has no choice, he's struggling with a reality he has never seen. I can see it in your face, Herr Hitler. You are terrified within, but you will not admit it.

Hitler: I am not through yet. I did not surrender while I was alive, why should I surrender now?

Jesus: You will have your way in the end, but listen for now. God did not make you for ownership; He made you for surrender.

Hitler: I thought you said—

Jesus: I'm leading you one step at a time. He made you for surrender, Adolf—surrender first to Me. You are not your own. Even in the war that you were losing, you could not bring yourself to surrender. You see, in trying to own everything, you lost out. You can never own anything without selling something first. You never spend without exchanging, diminishing, or increasing value... You're silent, Adolf. Why?

Hitler: I'm thinking.

Jesus: Keep thinking. I'll wait.

Hitler: You never spend without exchanging, diminishing, or increasing value?

Jesus: Yes. And life is of essential value.

Hitler: That's where I think...that's where my definitions depart from Yours.

Jesus: That is exactly the truth. You reduced the value of human life to nothing more than mere matter that stood in your way.

Hitler: The philosophers changed Your definition of life, You know. The sciences proved You wrong. I mean, Darwin told us we were here by an accident of atoms. My fellow countryman, Nietzsche—by the way, I presented his works to Stalin and Mussolini. I was so proud that my fellow countryman had philosophized on this theory.

Jesus: You bought into a lie.

Hitler: Well, I remember what Nietzsche said about equality, that this whole business of human beings being equal is a lie concocted by inferior people. I remember his exact words: "The real truth about 'objective truth' is that the latter is a fiction. Truth must first be expressed in language, and language is notoriously unable to get us to reality."

Jesus: That's not all he said.

Hitler: I know. He went on to say: "Words, like a hall of mirrors, reflect only each other and in the end point to the conditions of their users, without having established anything about the way

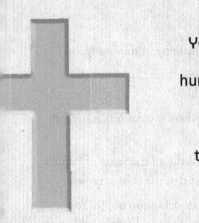

You reduced the value of

human life to nothing more

than mere matter

that stood in your way.

—Jesus

things really are." Then he added this: "Truth is the name we give to that which agrees with our own instinctive preferences."

Jesus: That's still not all he said.

Hitler: All right then, *you* end it!

Jesus: He ended that by saying, "I am still too pious that I even worship at the altar where God's name is Truth." Adolf, he knew his lie was unlivable and tried to smuggle in truth in order to survive. No wonder he went insane! Nietzsche knew the entailments of reducing human life to matter and so to increase his own value was forced to cling to the alternate "truth" that some have more value than others. Did you hear Me?

Hitler: Please explain what You're saying.

Jesus: If you reduce mankind to mere matter, the offspring of natural causes, you take away the equality and dignity of each person. That is why I asked the philosophers to look into the face of a little child, for to such belongs the kingdom of heaven. I want to tell you of something tragic.

Hitler: Why should I care to hear it?

Jesus: Hours after you died, Joseph Goebbels's wife, Magda, with the help of doctors, poisoned her six children before she and her husband killed themselves. Six little ones! Six more among thousands of others sacrificed for a political scheme. Your violence was the logical outworking of your view of humanity.

Bonhoeffer: This is something the naturalists never thought about.

Jesus: To some extent they did. They spoke some about the violence that would come as a result of reducing human life to natural causes. They just didn't have the spiritual discernment to understand the hell they were introducing into the world by taking away the laws of God and destroying the sacredness of life.

Bonhoeffer: I remember reading Darwin and Nietzsche. Both talked about the violence that would result from their theories because nature was "red in tooth and claw."

Jesus: Yes, but the inheritors of their philosophy did not call it by name. Professing themselves to be wise, they too became fools. They invented terms and slogans that hint at freedoms while actually enslaving. By changing words, they thought they could change reality. The millions of innocent lives that have been lost in ethnic discriminations against color and creed are terrifying to even imagine, yet that is the legitimate offspring of a worldview based on natural causes. And if that's the way of nature, why should politics be any different? They never answered the question of how it is possible to make moral judgments in a world with no moral law. The greatest price they pay is with their children. Adolf, your actions were the logical out-workings of a lie!

Bonhoeffer: Jesus, I have one question for You. By offering him forgiveness if he repents, are You giving him a second chance?

Jesus: You will see and understand.

Hitler: Before I make my case, I must ask a question.

Jesus: You have your moment now.

Hitler: I'm puzzled. I thought You clearly told Your disciples that politics and religion don't mix. Why did You raise up an underground movement among the clergy to plot against me, the political leader?

Jesus: Where did I say that politics and religion don't mix?

Hitler: Didn't You say that Your kingdom was not of this world?

Jesus: Yes, but that is not all that I said when I spoke to Pilate.

Hitler: What else did you say?

Jesus: I said that any power that he had was only temporary and part of an eternal plan. This is what kings and leaders do not seem to understand. Politics and trust in God must speak to each other. Disbelief in God can legitimize anything in the name of politics. But to politicize religion by forcing it upon people and using political power to engender belief is a false kind of belief.

Hitler: Then how do politics and religion speak to each other?

Jesus: You've asked a most difficult question. While religion cannot be politicized, to evict faith in God from the laws of the land or to forbid teaching faith in God to our children is to create a society one generation from total anarchy. Demagogues and anarchists are always in the wings to seize that power. Laws are fragile things that attempt to make up for the weaknesses of the human heart. When I called My people, the Jews, from bondage into the Promised Land, I first redeemed them. Then I gave them the law and finally I taught them how to worship. They forgot the first power I offered them.

Hitler: What was that?

Jesus: That it was I who redeemed them. You cannot have a law in any land that will bring peace until the heart has been redeemed. The sting of death is sin, and the strength of sin is the law.

Hitler: I'm not sure what that means.

Jesus: No, you never have, and that's why you keep talking about forgiveness without knowing why it's even needed. Sin is like a sting imbedded in the soul. When you turn to the law for help, it only intensifies the pain of the sting, and death is the result. You must get the sting out. Sin must be extracted so that the law can point beyond itself to life. Redemption of your soul is the price that was paid to restore its original value that had been traded away for lawless things. I told you before that if you did not understand the true worth of your soul, you would barter it away for far less than it's worth.

Hitler: But how does that change the world of politics?

Jesus: You cannot love the law for its own sake. Politics governs society, but the moral law must govern politics. Law and justice are not the same, you know. This is why I alone can take a life, for I alone, as just and the justifier, can restore it. This is also how those who follow Me play an all-important part in the politics of a nation. Have you ever tasted salt?

Hitler: Of course.

Jesus: Locked into salt is the power to penetrate, to season, and stem rot. My church is intended to be salt. The penetration of society and culture by the church must come from within. The church cannot isolate itself from the society it inhabits. It must participate from within the society, changing hearts one by one.

Hitler: That is a very slow method.

Jesus: But it's the way of love and the way of true change.

You manufactured light to create a false aura about you. I am true light and My church must reveal the darkness by shining into the darkness and demonstrating the difference between darkness and light. Salt and light—one works from within the society and the other from without. That is the ethic of the kingdom, an ethic that changes the heart by My power and demonstrates what life was meant to be with My love.

Hitler: I never did understand this kind of thing. I mean, the church I'm familiar with operated its own politics and bartered its own international agreements.

Jesus: I know. The history of the church is not always a beautiful one. Many who have named My name never knew Me. And they have faced their own judgment.

But now, Adolf, it is your turn to explain why you rejected Me, not complain of how others misrepresented Me. The truth is that you never sought Me. You wanted to rule the world. In a greater or lesser way, each person faces the temptation to redefine the world according to his or her own terms. But life must be seen in its eternal splendor, not in its temporal indulgence.

Hitler: Okay, for the sake of argument, if redemption is the first step, where does Your law come in?

Jesus: The reconciliation of liberty with law can be accomplished only when the heart is in tune with a higher law than merely man's law. When a people who have recognized their sin turn to God's grace, His law is seen as defining for the soul and for the well-being of a nation. Without redemption the law serves only to condemn them and draw attention to their shortcomings.

I gave My law to My people as a guide for them to follow and obey if they were to prosper in their new land. They were to be an example to the world of what a people who live by God's law look like. But from the beginning I knew they would never be able to keep the law that they had pledged allegiance to.

Hitler: If You knew they would never be able to keep it, why ever did You give it?

Jesus: So they could see what was in their hearts and turn to Me, the only one who can empower them to keep the law. Your judges who were tried at Nuremberg heard these words when their sentences were passed: "Justice, truth, and the value of life must be at the heart of all law." That is what I write on the heart that has been redeemed. There is no law powerful enough to change the human heart from being self-serving.

Hitler: Why didn't You just offer Your help in the first place?

Jesus: It's not enough to command love; it must be wooed. When I died on the cross, I laid down My life to invite you to share My love. I suffered it all because sin had to be revealed for what it is and the penalty of sin paid. Only then could you be forgiven and spared from eternal judgment. When I went to the cross, I cried out for the forgiveness of those who crucified Me because they represented all of humanity and I represented the heart of God. God's grace is the only cure for humanity's sin. When you killed and brutalized people, you made certain that you weren't there to hear their screams. Now you're going to hear those screams, and they will haunt your eternity with remorse and anguish.

Hitler: Wait a minute! I thought we were going to discuss my forgiveness.

Jesus: We're not through yet.

Hitler: Why do I get the feeling that part of the torture of my heart is going to be in not knowing…

Jesus: In not knowing what love is? You never loved anyone, Adolf. You only used people and your relationships with them. Hell is being totally separated from God, the source of all love. My love and peace I offer to everyone who comes to Me. It is a love and peace that the world cannot give.

Hitler: Even as You speak, I'm thinking about something

Napoleon said. Yes, I know he tried to separate himself completely from Your rule, and the changes he brought to Europe last to this day. But he said something that haunted me in my early days.

Jesus: Go ahead and quote it to remind yourself of what is true.

Hitler: He said that his kingdom, Caesar's kingdom, and Alexander's kingdom would all come to nothing because they were based on power and presence. He, Caesar, and Alexander had to be there and wield power to ensure the compliance of the people. But Your kingdom, he said, would continue because it was based on the laws of love and on a different kind of power.

Bonhoeffer: Can I add something here that just rises within me? Your comment, Herr Hitler, about a changed Europe…I recall making a statement that America was the only nation that wrote its constitution while bearing in mind the depravity of man. How critical it was in its formation.

Jesus: Yes, but America is forgetting that now, too.

Hitler: Those truths the church claims to hold, then, will be lost, won't they, as the government wields more power over it?

Jesus: No, that will never happen. I am always present with My followers. I will not leave them. My presence lives in them. They do not fear death because I have conquered the grave. I am with them to the end.

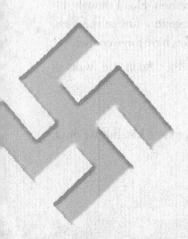

Lift your eyes to parts of the

world where the church is

growing, places where

tyrants have tried to kill it

and destroy My Word.

But My Word abides forever

and rises up to outlive

its pallbearers.

—Jesus

Just lift your eyes to parts of the world where the church is growing, places where tyrants have tried to kill it and destroy My Word. But My Word abides forever and rises up to outlive its pall-bearers.

Hitler: You said something earlier that I didn't understand. I think You said that evil must be exposed and that this is what the law has accomplished. I'm not sure what You mean by that.

Jesus: Evil breaks, destroys, distorts. Evil brings suffering.

Bonhoeffer: Herr Hitler, this is the heart of the gospel you rejected. You never understood what true sacrifice is. It is infinitely easier to suffer with others than to suffer alone. It is infinitely easier to suffer as public heroes than to suffer apart and in ignominy. It is infinitely easier to suffer physical death than to endure physical suffering. Jesus suffered as a free man—alone, apart, in ignominy, in body and in spirit. His sacrifice was the result of evil. His resurrection is what makes our fellowship with God possible. You never understood true sacrifice or true hope.

Hitler: So, there remains just one last question. Had I thought I needed to repent of anything at the last second—I mean the very last second before I came here—would You have forgiven me?

Jesus: I would like to take you to My Father, Adolf. He awaits all who will come to Him. Just follow Me.

Bonhoeffer: May I come too?

Jesus: Walk beside Me, Dietrich. Adolf, follow Me. But we must enter into My Father's presence through a very narrow door, so follow Me closely, Adolf.

Hitler: Don't walk too fast or too far ahead of me. I lose the light and this place is getting darker as we get closer to the door. Can't You slow down? Slow down!

Jesus: Keep your eye on the door, Adolf, because there is only one door. Are you sure you want to be forgiven?

Hitler: I want to see what really happens. I cannot see a door. You seem to be changing form as if You Yourself are a door.

Jesus: Keep following Me closely and you will find out what that means. I ask you again, Adolf Hitler: Do you know how a person is forgiven? Do you understand the cost and impact of forgiveness for you? Do you understand what it cost Me and how it must change you?

Hitler: I can't hear You clearly anymore. Can't You speak up? I seem to be brushing past people who want to hold on to me. What is happening?

Jesus: Keep your eye on Me, Adolf!

Hitler: Who was that? Who was that I just saw?

Jesus: You've met him before. He became your downfall. He will be seeing Me next. He too wants to know what would have happened if he had repented and asked Me for forgiveness before he died. We have almost reached the point into the eternal. Keep your eye on Me, Adolf!

Hitler: But wait! Was that Stalin? Was that Josef Stalin I saw? Why that butcher, that schemer, that destroyer of my dreams! Surely You're not planning to give him any forgive—

Bonhoeffer: Jesus, what happened? We lost him! I heard the floor give way!

Jesus: There is no second chance here, Dietrich. The only thing that happens before they meet their destiny is a confirmation in their own hearts that they do not understand what forgiveness means and how a forgiven person lives. Nor do they want it.

Bonhoeffer: It's as if the earth itself opened up and the weight of his own unbelief—

Jesus: Welcome, Dietrich, My child. Enter into the joy of the Lord. Here there are no more tears, no more sorrow. Death itself is swallowed up in victory for those whose hearts are surrendered to My Father.

Bonhoeffer: I am at a loss for words!

Jesus: And that is your only loss!

EPILOGUE

The Indian sage Acharya Vinoba Bhave said that in the premodern world, violence was relative. In the modern world, he said it would become absolute. That was quite a statement to have made decades ago. What does it mean, that violence is absolute? It means that violence would become the governing ethic for a world in which all seek ascendance. Hitler was just a representative of the human heart when violence has become absolute.

I urge the reader to see the two movies *Nuremberg* and *Judgment at Nuremberg*. In that microcosm the immensity and tragedy of the human predicament become evident: In denying the moral law, everything becomes a pathetic attempt to defend even the abominable. In our world today, struggling with Al Qaeda and those who try to justify their evil ways, there is little difference. Anytime a worldview seeks to govern by force, this is the result. Nor is there a difference in the devaluing of life that we see even in so-called free societies. The atrocities we commit in our civilized societies are only dressed up with law and language. The world is reeling with the tricks being played to justify the profane. Our ways today are only better than sixty years ago at the surface level. At the core we are in the same mess.

That is why Jesus never sought to bring in His kingdom by our means. His is neither a pure democracy nor an imposed autocracy. He sought to win the hearts of men and women who in turn will live their lives conformed to the image of God's Son, respecting the intrinsic dignity of each individual person and understanding true freedom. But that is not as simple as it may sound.

In the Bible, there is an interesting conversation between Jesus and the Pharisees. A group of them came to Jesus and said, "We know you're a man of integrity and you teach the way of God according to the truth. Tell us then what is your opinion? Is it right to pay taxes to Caesar or not?"

This was truly a trick question because they hated the yoke of Rome. But at the same time it was a real question. "Can you legitimize paying money to a pagan power?" "What do you do when your faith is violated by the powers that deny you the value of your own faith and of life itself?"

Jesus' answer was brilliant, but like many of His answers there was intentional subtlety so that only those who really sought the truth would find it. He asked for them to show Him a coin. "Whose image is this on the coin?" he asked.

"Caesar's," they answered.

"Then give to Caesar what is Caesar's and to God what is God's," Jesus said.

If you ponder that answer, you have the answer to politics. The coin may have Caesar's image on it, but whose image does the person who asked the question bear? The Pharisees missed the point. So did the Nazi officers who justified everything by saying they were "giving to Caesar what belonged to Caesar."

Humanity was not made in the image of Caesar, but in the image of God. That is a uniquely Christian truth. When we understand that, we understand what it means to frame a government and write laws that reflect that basic truth. No other worldview holds to that. We are made in God's image, but we have marred it. So those of us who castigate Hitler must realize that the castigation itself buys into the Judeo-Christian worldview that each human being has essential value because he or she has been made in the image of God. You simply cannot condemn Hitler without affirming the fundamental premise that life at its core is sacred.

And only in the person of God through His Son can we see the image we were meant to reflect. The hatred that tried Him and put Him to death was not accidental. Nor is the natural inclination in all of us throughout all ages to put Him away (or as the Bible says, to repeatedly crucify Him and put Him to open shame) accidentally. For with Him out of the way, there is no absolute standard we can follow. And each person can then do and be what is right in his or her own eyes. But in His willingness to die by His own will, He has restored to us the unmarred image that we were meant to have. It took His death to show us our hearts, and it took His resurrection to rescue us from ourselves and show us the way out of our dilemma.

The Lamb talks to the Führer to point the way back for all of us, for we have all killed God's image and find ways of hating while justifying it. The Lamb shows the way of loving by just means. Until we see in each one of us the same capacity for evil as Hitler had, we will never see the possibility of Jesus in all of us. The Third Reich meant control from the outside by fear. The Rule of God means peace on the inside by the incentive of love. Outside of Jesus Christ there is no possibility of true freedom and intrinsic worth. That is why He said, "I have come that you might have life."

For Hitler, who denied the image of God, the ends justified the means, and the ends were spelled by the supremacy of some men over others. That was his reich, his kingdom. Dietrich Bonhoeffer, who affirmed the image of God, knew that the means had to justify themselves because without that, any ends could be justified and any means employed to destroy the value of human life. That was the true reich, the true kingdom to be pursued. Jesus showed the only means to the ends for which we were made. Beginning with the poor in spirit and ending with the pure in heart, the kingdom is attained, for that is God's kingdom. Only in Jesus could both Hitler and Bonhoeffer have recognized the problem and found the solution. And so we pray, "Thy kingdom come, O Lord—in our hearts first before we see it in the world."

NOTES

1. Hitler's Final Political Testament is found on a number of websites. The link I used is www.humanitas-international.org/holocaust/htestmnt.htm (from The Holocaust Project).

2. Bernstein's story is told in Sara Tuvel Bernstein, *The Seamstress: A Memoir of Survival* (New York: G. P. Putnam's Sons, 1997).

3. Altner's story is told in Helmut Altner, *Berlin Dance of Death* (Havertown, PA: Casemate Publishers, 2002).

4. Dietrich Bonhoeffer, *Letters and Papers from Prison, Enlarged Edition* (New York: Touchstone, 1997), 347–48.

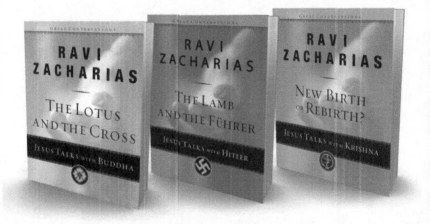

Jesus Talks to Oscar Wilde on the Pursuit of Pleasure

Why would God create us with such strong appetites for pleasure if He didn't intend for us to indulge them? Oscar Wilde gets to ask Jesus Christ this question in Ravi Zacharias's fictional dialogue—the second book in the dramatic Great Conversations series. Wilde, a witty author and conversationalist who committed his life to the pursuit of pleasure, is the ideal person to argue with Jesus about this perplexing issue. The two historical figures think out loud about beauty, Blaise Pascal, and the Bible in a sparkling interchange that will fascinate and enlighten readers.

WHY DO THEY CALL IT GOOD WHEN WE CALL IT EVIL?

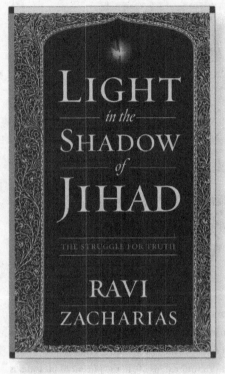

The terrorists who brought death to thousands said they did it in God's name. Thousands of Christians around the world gathered in churches to pray for peace, while others blamed the very idea of God for the tragedy. Ravi Zacharias deals with five of the major questions on people's minds after September 11:

- *Is this true Islam or a fanatical counterfeit?*

- *In what ways does the relationship between church and state change a nation's view of religion and affect its culture?*

- *Is religion dangerous to a culture?*

- *Was there a prophecy that this would happen?*

- *Where does this leave the future?*

HB 06.22.2020 1922

"If we find those answers," writes Zacharias, "they will spell life, steadying the soul even though the heart still aches."